MEMORIALS TO REMEMBER

*How to Plan, Prepare,
and Perform Funerals*

BILL FIX

ISBN: 978-1-7340046-1-8 (Paperback)

Scripture quotations primarily taken from *The Holy Bible, New International Version® NIV*® Copyright © 1973 1978 1984 2011 by Biblica, Inc. TM Used by permission.

Scriptures from the *King James Bible* are indicated as such.

Editing by DocEditing.com

My sheep listen to my voice; I know them, and they follow me.
I give them eternal life, and they shall never perish;
no one will snatch them out of my hand.
My Father, who has given them to me, is greater than all;
no one can snatch them out of my Father's hand.
John 10: 27-29

CONTENTS

Chapter One
HOW TO BE PREPARED

The knowledge I have gained from performing hundreds of funerals can be of huge benefit to others. Most officiants do an excellent job, but all of us could improve. This book provides advice for pastors or officiants who want to do a better job at conducting funerals.

A friend of mine, Pastor Richard Jewett, introduced me to the excellent opportunity open for clergy to officiate funerals for people without pastors or for those whose pastor has a scheduling issue and is too busy to perform a funeral. Although officiating funerals has become a source of income to help support my wife and I in retirement, it has become much more than that. I receive tremendous fulfillment as God opens the door for me to help families navigate through one of the most challenging times in their lives, the death of a loved one. Being called to do this is an honor and privilege. I find tremendous fulfillment in pursuing this calling because it is necessary.

I spend a significant amount of time on each service because I want to minister to the families in the best way that I can. I like to meet with each family personally and then organize the thoughts expressed during that meeting into a service. God has even given me the inspiration to write poems describing a part of each deceased person's journey. I am sharing one of the many poems I have written; feel free to use it by replacing the name or better yet, try writing one of your own.

Love You, Ann
by Pastor Bill Fix

The last days were hard as you struggled to breathe
We desired to do more as we prayed for your need.
It was such a surprise when you left and went on
But it is glorious to know that you've just gone home.

We walked with you often as you neared Heaven's Gates
You gave us some signs, nearing the end of your race.
We wish we could thank you for everything you have done
But we take comfort in knowing a great victory you've won.
So we are happy and sad and mixed up inside
But in our hearts, Ann, your memory resides.
Perhaps, it's "So long," but we'll see you again
We eternally love you Ann, our forever friend.

Consulting resources like this book is a part of preparation. This book provides a-step-by-step method for conducting a funeral service that has worked for me and is transferable for others who are called on to lead a funeral. Along with the methodology, I've also included examples of guidelines, ideas, tips, questions for families, and the steps that I take when planning, preparing, and performing a funeral.

Feel free to modify any part of this system or process to meet your unique needs. This proven system works well for me and I'm sure it will help simplify preparation and improve the outcome for you. Although every service will have differences, they will also share enough similarities to allow prior planning.

| Planning

The first funeral someone conducts establishes the realization that there is much to learn. Officiants usually walk away from their first funeral knowing they need to learn how to do it better. Services intended to remember the dead, comfort the grieving and cling to God's promises are in the public eye and require planning and practice. The main purpose of this booklet is to help officiants and participants think through and better plan funeral services. Simply reading through it and using it as a reference is a type of planning. Without planning, accomplishing the goals of a funeral service is difficult.

The old axiom, "Prior planning prevents poor performance," is very true when it comes to conducting a funeral service. My first experience as an officiant was at a funeral service for a man named Al. Al was a member of my church and a great friend that I'd loved like a brother. I'd desired to do an excellent job at remembering his extraordinary life. I'd wanted to speak words that would comfort, assure, and provide hope for Al's wife, family, and friends. The problem was that I'd known very little about conducting funerals. I'd felt unprepared as I was trying to put all of the pieces together. I didn't have a system, and although I had taken a couple of classes in seminary on the topic, I'd been ill-equipped for it at that time. I found myself taking a crash course trying to discover what to do, how to do it, and when to do it. Finding very few resources, I'd talked to pastors and friends who provided much appreciated advice. Although Allen's family thought the service was a beautiful tribute to his life, I'd immediately known that I needed to learn more about conducting funerals.

For many years, as I have increasingly been called upon to conduct funerals, I've learned a great deal. The ceremonies have taken place in churches, chapels, funeral homes, cemeteries and banquet halls. Although I do about fifty funerals a year, each one is unique, distinct from all the rest. Part of my job is to discover and then communicate each person's uniqueness.

Most of the funerals are for people I have never met. I do not know anything about them and can only perform these services by gathering information. Staying prayed up, prepared, and passionate about helping grieving families is very helpful while I collect information. The only way for me to get to know the person who has died is through the eyes of those who knew them.

| It's All in the Name

The word "funeral" refers to the rituals of death. Most people would explain a funeral as the service associated with the death of a person. Many people perceive a funeral as morbid. Using the word "funeral" is fine but when speaking with the family about their loved one and during the service when the deceased's loved ones and friends are present, it is wise to display great sympathy. Although it is acceptable to use the word funeral to describe the service, it's not the best description as I emphasize eternal life. In Scripture, Jesus confirms eternal life.

Jesus said to her, "I am the resurrection and the life. The one who believes in me will live, even though they die; and whoever lives by believing in me will never die. Do you believe this?" John 11:25, 26

In my previous book, *The Dead-End Road Devotional,* I wrote that "All earthly roads will end, but the journey always continues." Calling this service a celebration of life, a memory of life, or a memorial service seems more accurate and compassionate than using the word "funeral." I almost always begin the service by saying, "This is a celebration of life as we remember today the life of [deceased person's name]."

The service should always look at the past, recognize the present, and assure the audience of the future. Although hellfire and brimstone are real, I have never been prompted by the Holy Spirit to preach a hellfire and brimstone message at a funeral. Remember that nothing you say at this service will alter the destination or journey of the deceased. Allow me to repeat that sentence again because it is so important: Nothing you say at this service will alter the destination or journey of the deceased. That is why I like to talk about the hope we have in Jesus, heaven, eternal life, and the promises of the Bible.

The word "funeral" is connected to morbid thoughts. I rarely use it to describe the service. I prefer to call it a "celebration of life," "memorial," "commencement," or "graduation into eternity." All of these recognize the truth of Scripture, without nullifying the reality of grief and tremendous loss.

| Officiant Responsibilities

Death is not predictable, but it is inevitable. Without a plan for memorial services, clergy and churches are at a considerable disadvantage. Systems, strategies, and models reduce the stress of planning in the middle of an emotional crisis, as death usually is.

PREPARATION is complicated without a plan, and doubly so without much experience. Early in my ministry, I admit I did not know what to do. I had attended many services for family members and friends, but I did not have a set order of service. I did not know who would be involved and did not know what questions to ask the family. I needed a system, but did not have one. I was unsure of my responsibilities. I had authority but lacked competence and confidence. I knew I could handle it as long as I could figure out what exactly to do. I learned that personal preparation could be complicated and stressful without a plan.

TIME MANAGEMENT is complicated because there is much to do and not much time to do it. When someone dies, a service is usually held within three or four days. Without a plan, much of this time can go by very quickly. As the window of time shrinks, stress levels run high. When an officiant lacks sufficient time to prepare, stress is the result.

Most people are surprised by death. SCHEDULES are already full. During this time, several activities are immediately added to the list of responsibilities. Items on the to-do list get moved around to accomplish tasks associated with the death. Significant time-consuming tasks that were already on the schedule still need to be completed. When responsibilities are suddenly added to an already full schedule, stress levels increase.

When the ultimate responsibility of making the service happen is yours, SMOOTH COORDINATION of people and events is necessary. Others may be called on to sing, read, or conduct a portion of the service. Details can be daunting. Will the singer need a piano accompaniment? Will they need a CD player? Will they need a cord to plug their cellphone into the public address system? Do they need a particular type of microphone? Assuming the musician has thought through all of these needs can often end poorly. When the church provides a meal for the family and their guests, many people are involved and coordinating the meal is a huge task. Considering all of these details before a death occurs is the best way to minimize stress and coordinate people.

Officiating a celebration or memorial of a person's life is a tremendous privilege and honor and also a great responsibility. An inexperienced officiant will experience added stress, but God is our helper and we can do this. OWN THE RESPONSIBILITY.

| Responsibilities of the Funeral Home Director

Families usually contract with a funeral home to provide services that will prepare their loved one's body for burial or cremation. Although the funeral home is a business, it offers a needed service to families making final arrangements concerning their deceased loved one. As a family enters into a contractual agreement with a funeral home, the services they provide are numerous.

The funeral home arranges transportation of the body to the funeral home.

A funeral home director meets with the family to finalize arrangements. Typically, the officiant will not attend this meeting but at times I've been asked to attend to lend support or to advise a widow, widower, single parent or very emotional informant. The funeral director's meeting with the family has three primary purposes: To gather information about the deceased, to make choices and determine next steps, and to determine the cost and payment method for the funeral home's services. The officiant may also request this information from the funeral director.

Information the director will collect includes:

- full name and other names used by the loved one, legal or otherwise
- birth date and place of birth
- death date and age of the deceased
- a listing of close relatives and friends of the deceased preceding them in death
- a listing of close relatives and friends of the deceased surviving them at the time of their death

Necessary choices and arrangements include:

- choosing the date and location of the viewing and services
- choosing embalming or cremation
- choosing the cemetery or the destination of the cremains
- choosing the burial vault type from several options
- choosing the casket or urn from many styles and price ranges
- determining the number of death certificates needed
- making arrangements to deliver clothing for the deceased
- determining hairstyle desired (recent photo is helpful)
- choosing keepsakes, if desired (for example, thumbprint jewelry)
- choosing a grave marker
- choosing an officiant to perform the ceremony (if not already chosen)
- determining whether an obituary listing will be published in the newspaper

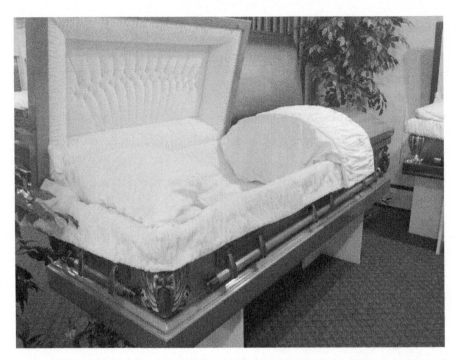

The funeral director will guide each family in the proper casket selection. Long caskets are available to accommodate taller people and shorter caskets are available to accommodate short people. Wider caskets are made to accommodate more robust people and child and infant caskets are also available. Most caskets are designed for viewing the body. The body is lifted up and raised for easier viewing. Before closing the casket, the body is lowered using a cranking device. Most caskets also have a cranking device that tightens the casket door and sets the seal.

Life insurance, social security, veteran benefits, loans, cash, credit cards, etc. are examples of payment methods for funeral home services. If the deceased person had already made pre-arrangements, a funeral home director will meet with the family and review the prearrangements. Numerous benefits can result from this pre-needs or pre-arrangement meeting:

- locking in the cost
- allowing for pre-payment (payment plans are available)
- allowing time to think through options and make wise choices

- enabling the person's wishes to be stated and honored, removing all doubts about the deceased's desires
- reducing stress both financially and mentally for family members

The funeral home

- prepares the body for burial or cremation.
- schedules visitation and service times in coordination with the funeral home schedule, the family's wishes, and the clergy, priest or cleric performing the service.
- files legal papers and orders death certificates as requested by the family.
- coordinates the services of the cemetery or crematory.
- places pictures, gifts, and flowers at the viewing, to be displayed.
- provides cards and a guestbook as requested.
- collects money for a charity or cause at the request of the family.
- coordinates hearse and limousine services.
- sometimes provides aftercare grief counseling.

The local papers will receive an obituary if requested by the family, but this is not a free service. It can be quite expensive. Often the funeral home will post the obituary on their website for anyone to print out as a keepsake.

| Reasons for Developing a Funeral System in the Church

Many people might say that funeral services are for the deceased. While the service is *about* the deceased, it is actually *for* those in attendance. The person that has died will be remembered and honored, and stories about them will be shared, but the benefit is for those attending the service. Well prepared churches have a written document listing the details in a step-by-step process. Systems may be unique to each church due to staffing and volunteer availability.

Five important reasons for creating a procedure:

- To reduce the possibility of forgetting an important detail. Putting much of the detail in checkable list form will provide a checklist to help prevent oversight. Using the list provides direction and instills confidence.
- To assist the officiant in meetings with the funeral director and the deceased's family. Having a list of questions ready to ask will help with establishing necessary details for behind-the-scenes activity and the ceremony.
- To group tasks into specific segments, making delegating work easier. Mini-checklists can be incorporated within the entire procedure for the building, kitchen, clean-up, greeting, music, meetings, etc.
- To make critical leaders aware that their services are needed and what those services are. If necessary, they can engage their volunteer base to get the job done and delegate authority and responsibility to critical people.
- To trigger activity that will ensure the building and equipment are ready for the service. Building readiness requires much more than cleaning. Seating may need to be set-up or rearranged. Drum sets, microphone stands, and other things may need to be disconnected and moved off the platform. Signs may need to be changed, and the fellowship hall may need set-up.

| Receiving Calls about Impending or Actual Death

I believe God helps members of the clergy when they receive a call about a death. These calls come in various forms and ways. When a family member calls, it is often a cry for spiritual help and support. As a pastor, I have received hundreds of these calls. Each one is a little different. Often, the family member is calling for the pastor to go to where the family is.

One of the most humbling calls for me to receive is from a person who seems to be full of life who asks me to perform their funeral. They usually ask to meet with me privately. When they ask whether I would conduct the service when they die, I always tell them it would be an honor and a privilege to do so.

Terri, a healthy-looking, middle-aged woman, asked to meet with me, one day. I was somewhat shocked when she asked me if I would perform her service when she died. Asking the question was awkward for her. She told me that she had a lung disease that would eventually take her life. I tried to be very gracious and told her I would be praying that God would extend her years. I thanked her for giving me the honor of remembering her life after her death. I encouraged her to share her wishes with her family member(s) so that whenever the time came, they could carry out her wishes. Several years later, I officiated her funeral. By then, she was one of my closest friends, and I loved her like a sister.

A church member asked if I would go with him to the hospital to visit his friend who was dying. When we'd arrived, I met his friend who had been a jockey. During a race years before, he had suffered a terrible accident that necessitated the amputation of his legs. The internal injuries from that accident had continued to plague this man. He was a talker and a jokester and when I'd arrived, he had not appeared to be a man who was dying but a man full of life. He laughed and told stories. He also confessed he had made many mistakes and during that visit, recommitted his life to Christ. He'd told me he was going to die soon. I had not believed it would be anytime soon because he'd been so full of life. I enjoyed hearing about his life as a father, husband and jockey. He told me of his love for his estranged family and his trust and belief in Jesus. I promised him I would be back the next morning. Then he asked me if I would do his funeral. I told him it would be my privilege and honor. Before I was able to return the next day, my new jockey friend died. I remember he'd been so looking forward to being free again. I conducted his Homegoing Celebration the way he'd wanted it to be.

Ray and his family, including his mother-in-law, had been attending my church. Late one night, Ray's mother-in-law died. When I'd received the call, I knew that he wanted me to be with them as her body was picked up. Different family members sat with her until the transport service arrived. I called everyone in the house to that room, and I thanked God for this dear woman's life and what she'd meant to all who knew her. I prayed for God to comfort the grieving family. We all left the room as the transport service wrapped her body for transport. After the transport service had removed the body, I prayed again with the family. After the prayer, they asked me if I would officiate the funeral service. I told them it would be my honor to do so. Although there were a lot of things I needed to know before the funeral, I did not ask any service-related questions that night.

The critical thing to remember on the initial call is to be empathetic, honored to be asked, and sensitive to the desires of the family. I received a call from a family asking me to conduct the funeral for Don, the patriarch of their family. Don was a beloved member of my church and a dear friend of mine. I immediately told them that I was sorry for their loss. I assured them that I valued their father's friendship, and it was my honor to do the service for the family.

Often I have been at the bedside with individuals as they have breathed their last breath on earth. It is such an emotionally moving time and it is a privilege to offer a prayer for family and friends at that moment. As we hold hands in a semi-circle around the loved one's bedside, I pray a prayer of thanksgiving for the person's life and influence. I often thank God that the battle is over and the victory won. I pray for good memories and grand thoughts. After the prayer, I avail myself to the family as a helper and resource for the next steps, if they so desire. I ask if they need assistance making a call to the funeral home of their choice or with making final arrangements, or help with packing up and taking things to their car. Whatever they need, I try to help. I do not hurry them but gently move them forward to the next steps. If they are alone, I might offer to drive them home.

A doctor, officer, or coroner pronounces the person deceased. If this takes place in a hospital or care facility, the body is cleaned up, all life support and monitoring machines are disconnected, and the family usually waits outside the room as this is happening. Most often, family members desire to be with the deceased for a while before going home. Sometimes the wait is considerable as close family members arrive. Eventually, family members go back to their homes. They begin making calls to notify others, and they think about the final arrangements. People make plans and grieve in different ways. Most of the time, I do not follow them to their homes unless they are all alone and need me. If they are all alone, I might sit with them until other family members or friends show up to help and support them. During conversations, they almost always ask me to do the service.

One evening, I was with a man in the hospital as he received a diagnosis of stage four cancer. I will never forget it. He, his wife, and I had been in the room when the doctor told him he probably had thirty to ninety days to live. In shock, I prayed with them after the diagnosis. We talked extensively about God being in control. We talked until I had to leave. I joked with him about ordering me breakfast the next morning because I was going to stop in to see him. Moments before I'd arrived the next morning, my friend died. The hospital had not yet notified his wife. I asked them to allow me to go to her home and tell her. When she answered the door and saw me, before I could say a word, she'd said, "He's gone, isn't he?" I drove her to the hospital to spend some time with him before the funeral home arrived to take his body away. As she was all alone, I stayed with her until her daughter arrived from seventy miles away. Before I left them, they asked me to perform the funeral. I told them it would be a great honor.

With a growing population of people who do not attend church or have a pastor, in times of death, someone may be referred to me, or the funeral home may call me on their behalf to ask if I would conduct the funeral service. If at all possible, I graciously accept the request.

My family extends far beyond siblings to include aunts, uncles, cousins, and more. It is not uncommon for me to receive a call from one of them when a family member passes. I always try to be there for them and graciously accept their request for me to do the funeral service.

Regardless of the circumstances, I try to graciously accept any call that I receive requesting me to do a funeral. I have decided to avail myself to conduct funerals because I want to comfort, encourage, and challenge people to believe in God, cling to the hope we have in Jesus, and live life to the fullest. I try to give people the benefit of the doubt and see the good in every person.

| Remaining Strong in the Middle of Emotion

I do not separate myself from emotion. My heart often beats with great grief, and I fight to hold back the tears. I am not always successful. I focus on serving families at one of their most emotional times of pain and need. My spirit grieves as I see a devastating loss. I've been there to officiate the services for two small children after they were tragically killed in an accident; when three small children were crying at their mother's casket after she had overdosed one final time; when a spouse openly grieved the death of the love of his life; when parents in shock buried their young son, a victim of gang violence; when parents of a son who'd had cerebral palsy watched him die; and when a twelve-year-old stood beside the casket of his friend who had drowned in a local pond.

At times, I become deeply grieved and tear up. Although I am deeply saddened and moved, I desire to share the hope of knowing Jesus. I want to be a comfort to those feeling the most significant loss. I want to help people remember that God is good and loving. I want them to remember the best things about the deceased. I want God to use me to reveal Him and His love even in times of great pain. I ask God for strength, and he helps me.

Prayer is something I often do on the run, but as I go through life, I need to take time out to seek God, get direction, and get my thinking right. When it comes to pastoring, counseling, officiating, and preparing services, there are many things to pray for and about.

I pray for myself. I want wisdom that comes from God. I need to display understanding, patience, guidance, strength, insight, love, faith, peace, and joy, and I realize I need to ask God for these things. I pray that God would give me eyes to see all things, including this great loss, as He sees them. I pray for strength and the skills I need to help others in the name of Jesus.

I pray for others. When I am leading a funeral service, I pray for those who will be assisting me with the service, the song leaders, the readers, the funeral director, and staff.

I pray for the family of the deceased and those grieving his/her death. I pray that God would give them ears to hear the message and that they would move closer to God.

Chapter Two

HOW TO BE PROFESSIONAL AND ORGANIZED

An ordered schedule of things that will occur during the service is called an order of service. The following order of service is an example that you can use as a guide to put together an order of service. Some denominations and faiths have step-by-step guidelines for officiants to follow. A Catholic service will differ from a Protestant service. A Lutheran service differs from a Baptist service. Some families desire to have a lot of music, while others may not want any. Sometimes secular music is chosen; other times, Christian music is chosen. The officiant may be the only one to speak at the service or may share the service with members of a group, such as the military, Masons, or the Moose. The family may desire another person to do a large portion of the service. The officiant's role is flexible as there are no hard and fast rules. All services are different.

The ORDER OF SERVICE below should be considered as an example, not standard. Each situation is a little different, so be ready, be flexible, and be Christlike.

Equipment check

It should go without saying that equipment needs to be working correctly to have a smooth service. Microphones, sound, and video equipment must be tested for two reasons. One, to make sure it works, and two to make sure the technician knows how to operate the equipment. Both are essential for a smooth service.

Prelude music (optional)

Music played before the beginning of the service is considered prelude music. It may include live music with musicians, singers, or pre-recorded music. Prelude music often reflects the kind of music the deceased enjoyed. Other times the family may choose to play Christian or religious music to respect the integrity of the service. For some, the service is a special holy moment; for others, it is a time to celebrate the life of the deceased.

Beginning announcement

An announcement is made, often by the funeral director or pastoral staff, with vital information regarding the service. Sometimes the announcement is detailed, other times it may be brief. Examples:

- Ladies and gentlemen, may I have your attention, please.
- In just a few moments, our services today to remember the life of (deceased's name) will begin here at (location).
- If you have a cell phone, would you please turn it off or silence it, so that it does not interrupt our service today.
- If you are going to join in the procession to the cemetery after our service here at (location), we want to remind you to keep your bright lights on and stay close to the vehicle in front of you, so there are no significant gaps between the cars.
- Immediately following the services at (final location), the family invites everyone to a (dinner or luncheon) in loving memory of the (deceased's name). The reception will take place at (location).

First song (optional)

Although prelude music may have been played, this song would be considered the first song of the service. Often, the deceased's favorite song is played, but it could be any song chosen by the family. If the service is at the deceased person's church, the first song can be a congregational song led by the church songleader. This first musical arrangement can be live or pre-recorded.

Welcome and introduction

Welcome people on behalf of the family and thank them for their support. Introduce yourself and explain your relationship with the deceased or your qualifications to lead the service. Introduce others, if you deem it appropriate: pianist, song leader, associate pastors, etc.

<u>Comforting scriptures</u>

Read a few comforting scriptures (others could participate in the service for this part). Many scriptures provide comfort. Here are a few of my personal favorites:

Jesus said, "Blessed are those who mourn, for they will be comforted." Matthew 5:4

He said, "Peace I leave with you; my peace I give you...Do not let your hearts be troubled and do not be afraid." John 14:27

Jesus said, "I am the resurrection and the life. The one who believes in me will live, even though they die; and whoever lives by believing in me will never die." John 11:25, 26

Let not your heart be troubled: ye believe in God, believe also in me. In my Father's house are many mansions: if it were not so, I would have told you. I go to prepare a place for you. And if I go and prepare a place for you, I will come again, and receive you unto myself; that where I am, there ye may be also. John 14:1-3 [King James Bible]

2 Thessalonians 2:15-17; Psalm 9:9, 18:28, 23:4; Isaiah 43:2, 49:13, 57:1-2

<u>Three reasons for gathering</u>

Possible reasons to list:

- To remember a good life – I often give a couple of examples relating to good things about the deceased.
- To comfort those who are grieving, the family and friends of the deceased – I remind people to email, call and visit them in the days, weeks, and months ahead. I tell them that grief is rarely for a day and sometimes lasts for years.

- To cling to the promises of God found in the Word of God –
  God has made many promises, including those just read. "Jesus
  has gone to prepare a place for us."

Prayer

This prayer time can reflect the purposes of the service, to remember
the deceased, to comfort the grieving, and to cling to the promises of
God. It can also be a sincere prayer for the hour that we have
gathered. It can be a prayer for peace amid confusion, joy amid grief,
and understanding amid uncertainty. It can be a prayer confessing the
mixed emotions that the people present are feeling, the sorrow in
their heart, and their trust in God. These examples are here to serve
as ideas only. Be creative!

Music selection (optional)

All of the music in this order of service is optional. If you decide to
insert a song here, live music would be best. Recorded music will
work, but it is not as well-received as live music. Another
congregation song is appropriate too.

Eulogy

The officiant usually delivers the eulogy. Sometimes, a family member
or close family friend may desire to read the obituary or do the eulogy.
The service is the most personable during the eulogy. Stories and
descriptions of the deceased in the eulogy will either make the
ceremony personally meaningful or it won't. The next chapter will
explore this portion of the service in depth. When a family member
decides to do the eulogy, I like to offer a few suggestions to help
them, if they are open to it.

Open microphone

During an open microphone segment of the service, the officiant
encourages family and friends of the deceased to give a testimony, tell
a short story about their loved one, or read a poem or letter that they
would like to share. Open microphone is an optional part of the
service. Some families do not want to open the service up to anyone
to share. In some cases, the family designates who will be permitted

to share, and the officiant introduces each one. If the family desires an open microphone, the officiant needs to caution the family. I almost always open the mic and usually have no problems at all, but unexpected things have happened.

A few things that have happened when I've opened the microphone to allow anyone to speak:

- They preached a sermon of their own.
- They shared multiple stories and spoke entirely too long.
- They shared a story that was already told by someone else.
- They approached the microphone under the influence.
- They were angry at the deceased and spoke unkindly.
- They called out other people they had a problem with, causing an argument.
- They made negative comments that discouraged others.
- They used vulgarity and profanity.
- They shared true but inappropriate stories.
- They became emotional and no one could understand them.

Poetry

Several beautiful poems could be shared. If the officiant, friends, or family members are inspired to write poems, they could be shared as well. Two poems that would fit well: "Footprints in the Sand" by Mary Stevenson, and "The Dash" by Linda Ellis. Other beautiful poems that would be appropriate to read in the ceremony can readily be found through a little research.

Music (optional)

A music selection just before the reading of scripture and the sermon message is very appropriate, especially if the music is live.

Scripture reading

Sharing scripture directly from the Bible is a powerful way to introduce the sermon. Many scriptures would be appropriate.

<u>Message</u>

This is not a time to beat people over the head with scripture. Instead, this is an excellent opportunity to exemplify and share the greatest command given to us by Jesus: "Love one another." At celebration of life services, I love to share scriptures and a message that declares, "God saves the best for last."

The following two messages are not complete in themselves but are examples of the types of sermons used for celebration of life services. Expand these thoughts to make them your own. They have worked well for me.

Sermon: Jesus Saves the Best for Last
John 2:1-11

The first recorded miracle of Jesus is a story of Jesus at a wedding feast. After the wine had run out, He turned water into wine. Life is like old wine. Old wine is excellent and adds to the significance of living. It represents joy and happiness. We foolishly believe life will last forever. But like the wine at the wedding feast, it runs out. Jesus made *new* wine, which was better than the first. Jesus offers a life that lasts forever and is just beginning when this life on earth suddenly closes its chapter.

Other interesting points in this passage:

Mary, Jesus's mother, told the servants to do whatever He said to do. We improve our quality of life when we do whatever He tells us to do.

This miracle took place at a wedding feast or banquet. The Bible speaks of a wedding banquet of a king for his son in Matthew 22:2-14. The Bible also compares Jesus to a bridegroom and describes the Church as His bride. The bridegroom is coming for His bride, and we have no idea when that will be.

Sermon: Eternal Rest

Jesus says in Matthew 11:28: "Come to me, all you who are weary and burdened, and I will give you rest."

We all get physically tired. I know the deceased did, I know I do, and I know you do too. I mean, eight to twelve hours of labor is tiring. Wouldn't you agree? Jesus's words become significant as He says, "Come to me, all you who are weary and burdened, and I will give you rest." God has provided us with sleep to replenish our bodies from physical tiredness. There are times when I need this rest.

There are other times when I cannot figure something out. I get stressed as I try to find a solution. I become mentally tired. Have you ever been mentally exhausted? Jesus says, "Come to me, all you who are weary and burdened, and I will give you rest." Just stepping away for a short time, I get replenished. I need to take a break or a time-out when I become mentally tired. How about you?

Some people wear me out, too. Have you ever met a negative person? Their negativity and pessimism indicates something is always wrong with their life. Do you know people like that? If I am around people like that for very long, I become exhausted and relationally tired. How about you? Do you ever get relationally tired? How about the deceased? Do you think they became relationally tired, too? Sure they did. That is why I am so glad Jesus says, "Come to me, all you who are weary and burdened, and I will give you rest."

We often experience physical, mental, and relational tiredness throughout life, and Jesus tells us, "Come to me, all you who are weary and burdened, and I will give you rest." These bodies wear out, and an exhaustion that we sometimes do not recognize may fall upon us. This happens when our earthly journey is winding down. His words are especially true in those times. "Come to me, all you who are weary and burdened, and I will give you rest."

This state is unlike physical rest, mental rest, or relational rest, for they are all temporary. But when we breathe our last breath, we enter into the presence of God, and He gives us eternal rest. He saves the best for last. He says, "Come to me, all you who are weary and burdened, and I will give you rest" (Matthew 11:28).

A few other scriptures among many that you could use for this portion of the service: Psalm 23; Isaiah 40:28-31; Luke 15:11-24; Ecclesiastes 3:1-8; John 14:1-3

Prayer

Prayer by the officiant. During this prayer, I often review what we have done during the service so far. We have remembered a good life. We have tried to comfort and encourage those who are grieving, and we have clung to the promises of God. We can thank God for being with us and providing comfort that only He can supply. We can thank Him for the hope that we all have in Jesus. And at the close of this prayer, I invite people to join me in praying the Lord's Prayer.

The Lord's Prayer

Invite everyone to join you in praying the Lord's Prayer. If we are going to the cemetery or the family has requested a short service and are not going to the cemetary, this would conclude my portion of the service at the church or funeral home.

Other groups (optional)

After concluding my portion of the service, if we are going to the cemetery and someone from a military, veterans, Masons, Moose, or any other group has a presentation, they will conduct their tribute next. If the select group presenting needs to go first, they may present after the "Beginning announcement" (third item in order of service). The military group, for example, may have another service to attend and ask to precede the officiant. The officiant needs to be flexible.

If we are not going to the cemetery and a group has a presentation, they will do it after the internment prayer.

Instructions for how to continue

If we are going to the cemetery, the funeral director will announce how we will continue. The funeral director will thank all those that participated in the service and tell the pallbearers to wait in a particular location. He will announce how the final pass by the casket or urn will occur and ask people to return to their cars, turn on their lights, and to keep a close but safe distance between participating cars when in procession to the cemetery. After the family has passed by the coffin, it is closed by the funeral director and the pallbearers carry it to the hearse.

The family usually chooses six strong individuals to serve as pallbearers. Caskets and bodies can be fairly heavy. Pallbearers carry the body to the hearse and from the hearse to the cemetery service chapel or graveside.

If we are not going to the cemetery, skip to "Final announcement," at which time the funeral director will give final pass-by instructions.

Loading the hearse

The officiant walks in front of the casket as the pallbearers carry the casket to the hearse.

Procession

The officiant will usually ride with the funeral director in the hearse with the hearse driver, or will drive his own vehicle to the cemetery.

Arrival at the cemetery

At the cemetery the officiant moves to the rear of the hearse and walks in front of the casket and pallbearers to the cemetery chapel or the graveside.

Prayer

Open this final portion of the service with prayer

Scripture reading

Use appropriate scripture readings of your choice

Words of encouragement

Final words of assurance, hope, and comfort

Poetry

Read or recite poem(s) or quotes of choice

Final internment prayer

Say an internment prayer of choice.

A military salute for a deceased veteran (option)

Representatives from a particular branch of service, the VFW, or the Veterans Association may take over the service at this point. A military service includes folding and presenting the American flag, playing taps, and a tribute with a three-volley salute.

Final announcement

Funeral director's closing announcement thanking participants and explaining final pass-by.

If the service continued at the cemetery, move on to "Vauting and burial," and if there was no continuance of the service at the cemetery because of cremation, inclimate weather, or family choice, move on to "Reception."

<u>Vaulting and burial (optional)</u>

Some families may desire to witness the vaulting of the casket and the burial. Other families may decide not to.

<u>Reception</u>

Family and participants drive to the reception, which can be a luncheon, dinner, or fingerfoods. The officiant often prays before the meal at the reception.

Chapter Four includes two examples of complete services.

Chapter Three
HOW TO BE UNIQUE AND PERSONAL

The best eulogies are very personal, and highlight the best parts of an individual's life. To craft numerous years into a brief summation is a real art. To make it happen, the officiant must gather accurate data from the funeral home, by meeting with family and close friends of the deceased, and by observing the pictures and memorabilia displayed by the family prior to the service.

The officiant receives a clergy card or clergy record and obituary from the funeral home. While meeting with the family, the funeral director collects information that they transfer to a clergy card and obituary. The clergy card or record is a quick summary of the facts covered in the obituary and should be kept on hand for a reference when meeting the family. It fits nicely in a suit pocket or within the pages of a book, such as a Bible or journal. I study the clergy card and use it to reference the names of family members when speaking to them.

The obituary includes all the facts found on the clergy record card, but is written in complete sentences and usually covers a full sheet of paper. Using the obituary as a quick reference is awkward, but is valuable when sculpting the eulogy.

Clergy record card

Following is an example of a clergy record card which is foldable to fit in a lapel coat pocket.

(left inside page)

Name: Random Anonymous

Residence: Taylor, MI

Date of birth: May 21, 1949

Place of birth: Pretendland, Arizona

Passed away: April 28, 2020

Age: _70_ years ___ months ___ days

Married to: Jessica Anonymous

Additional information:

                        (usually blank)

Clergy: Pastor Bill Fix

Date of service: May 4, 2020

                        Hour: 10 a.m.

Service: Journey Church

Visitation: May 3, 2020

                        Hours: 1-9 p.m.

                        at New Horizon Funeral Home

(right inside page)

Survived by:

Wife:	Jessica Anonymous
Son:	Freddy (Carol)Anonymous
Daughter:	Rosie (Charlie) Shoulda
Son:	Jerry (Sally) Anonymous
Parent(s):	Margie Anonymous
Brother:	Archie Anonymous
Sister:	Dorothy (Phil) Petel

Grandchildren: Suzie, Mike, Ariel, Shirl,

Archie, Martin

Preceded by:

Parent(s):	Horatio Anonymous
Brother:	Raymond Anonymous
Son:	Harold Anonymous

Grandchildren: Mark

Obituary

An obituary is written very similar to a news release. It is often placed on the funeral home's website and sometimes in the local newspapers.

Obituary for: Random Anonymous

May 21, 1949 – April 28, 2020

Random (Randy) Anonymous died April 28, 2020 at his home in Taylor, Michigan. Random was born May 21, 1949, in Pretendland, Arizona. Random is survived by his loving wife of 40 years, Jessica Anonymous and three children including two sons, Freddy married to Carol Anonymous and Jerry married to Sally Anonymous, and his precious daughter, Rosie married to Charlie Shoulda. Surviving Random is his dear mother, Margie Anonymous, a brother Archie Anonymous, and a sister Dorothy married to Phil Petel. Random is survived by six amazing grandchildren, Suzie, Mike, Ariel, Shirl, Archie, and Martin. He is preceded in death by his father, Horatio Anonymous, brother Raymond, a son Harold and a grandson Mark.

Random retired from the Ford Motor Company after 35 years of service. He loved his family and will be deeply missed by all who knew him. Visiting hours will be on May 3, from 1-9 p.m. at New Horizon Funeral Home and the memorial service will be held at Journey Church on May 4 at 10 a.m.

At times the obituary is read, word for word, as part of the eulogy. Most officiants, however, include information from the obituary, but not word for word.

The most valuable source for the personal information shared in the eulogy comes directly from the people who knew the person the best. Meeting with the deceased's close family and friends can provide the necessary information to make the eulogy personable. The informant is the person making the funeral arrangements with the funeral home and often the one paying the final bill. They have a vested interest in the service and prove to be very helpful in sculpturing the eulogy. If the only time to meet with family is during the visitation hours, it is best to find a private office or location. Otherwise, the family will feel obligated to get up and greet visitors coming in, and it becomes challenging to gather the information you need.

| The Family Meeting

Usually, the family meeting is informal and begins with introductions and prayer. I try to make the family feel comfortable. I write the questions down so that I do not miss anything that I need to ask.

I usually begin with a list of attributes, interests and descriptions that I simply check off. I tell them that I am going to give them a list of one word descriptions and I want to know if their loved one could be described this way or not. I also ask them to think of examples to support why they described their loved one this way.

__ loving	__ quiet	__ loud
__ kind	__ talkative	__ sharp
__ generous	__ encouraging	__ role model
__ faithful	__ organized	__ opinionated
__ strong-willed	__ pack rat	__ good cook
__ family	__ shopper	__ golf
__ sports	__ outdoors	__ bowling
__ hard worker	__ garden	__ traveling
__ other _____		

I ask a series of questions about their life:

Favorite music?
Favorite TV programs?
Favorite movies?
Did they like to travel? Where to?
Any hobbies or collections?

What did they love to do?
Favorite restaurants?
Favorite pets?
Where did they work?

I ask if they loved any of the following activities and if so, to what extent.

___ bowling   ___ woodworking   ___ boating

___ eating out   ___ social media   ___ gardening

___ crafts   ___ camping   ___ travel

___ playing cards   ___ hunting, fishing, hiking

___ cooking or baking   ___ cycling, walking, exercising

___ playing an instrument   ___ sewing, knitting, crocheting

___ other _____

Details about their education?
Any military service?
Any favorite sports teams?
What did they teach you personally?
How did they make you laugh? …feel proud? …encourage you?
Were there any sayings or phrases they would always use?
Family get-togethers, birthdays, graduations, weddings, etc.?
Were holidays special? How?
How did they encourage you and others?
What will you never forget about them?
Tell me about their Faith? Belief in God? Church? How they lived?
Any favorite Bible scriptures?
Any special friends?
Would you like me to thank anyone? Doctors, hospice staff, caregivers, etc.
Tell me about their home: welcoming? relaxed? immaculate? fun?

I explain how the service will begin with me thanking the guests on behalf of the family for their support and for being there as it means a lot. I tell them that I will introduce myself and use three short scripture passages to bring comfort from God's word.

I explain the three reasons why we gather and that we will be there to celebrate a life well lived, comfort the grieving, and cling to the promises of God.

I review the information provided by the funeral home on the clergy record card and obituary for accuracy and ask if everything is correct and if there are any additions. Generally half the time, people have forgotten someone that should have been in the obituary. I also ask for correct pronunciations of names and gender.

I ask if the deceased used any nicknames. If applicable, I ask what the grandchildren called them.

I ask if I have missed anything they desire me to say about their loved one.

I ask if anyone else would like to say a few words about the deceased or if they would like me to open up the microphone for others to speak.

If the service is going to be at the church, and the church will be providing a meal afterward, I ask how many they think will attend. (I will pass this information on to the meal coordinator at the church.)

I review the scheduled time for the visiting hours, service, and location.

I close the meeting by thanking the family for their time and praying for them. I give them a business card and tell them if they think of anything else to give me a call.

Three rules for creating the best eulogy:

1. Be personal – Tell people about the deceased
2. Be positive – Talk about the most positive things
3. Be brief – Keep the stories short and accurate. Lengthy stories do not go over well.

Gathering and organizing this information into a presentable format, if done correctly, will make the eulogy a very up close and personal part of the service.

As early as possible, I try to get the details for the funeral service from family and friends. I need to know the name of the deceased, where the service will be, date and time of the service, and a family contact name and number. I get all of this information from the funeral director or the family.

In my initial meeting with the family, I try to get to know them, and as I want them to feel comfortable with me, I try to learn their names. As I gather the stories, history, and details for the eulogy, I try to put the family at ease. I want them to feel comfortable around me.

Often, people ask if I think this person made it to heaven or not. As the officiant, my job is not to judge whether a person is in Heaven or Hell. I am not qualified to say. I do not even think it would be right to guess. I know of two stories in the Bible about people who had denied Christ, yet most believe are in Heaven. The thief on the cross, most likely bad to the bone, turned to Christ in his final moments, and Jesus said to him, "Today, you will be with me in Paradise." Peter, who'd said he would never deny Christ, denied Christ three times on the night of Christ's trial and pending crucifixion. I always focus all of my energy on pointing people to Jesus and the hope we have in Him.

At the visitation and before the service, I walk around and talk to as many people as I can. They tell me about their relationship to the deceased and sometimes a story or fact that I want to include in the service, usually the eulogy. For example, someone may say he was their favorite uncle or cousin. Someone else might say they were on the same golf team, or he attended his church and served as an usher. These kinds of side conversations are valuable eyewitness accounts that I can add in the eulogy.

If several people are in the ceremony, I meet with them collectively before service time to review the order of service and pray with them. I also provide the funeral director with a copy of the order of service.

| Burial Costs and Options

The financial strain of needed services related to the deceased can put tremendous stress on the person's remaining loved ones. Being knowledgable, concerning these expenses, is helpful. Knowing and understanding the options available can be an asset to families making final arrangements for a loved one. The stress often causes contention between surviving family members about how to pay for the services needed. At a time when a family needs no additional pressure, the reality of funeral costs may hit them hard. The average price for these services is estimated to be about $9,000. For most people, this is a significant and burdensome expense. Funeral prices vary considerably among funeral homes and geographic areas of the country. Following is a reasonable estimate for the main costs involved:

- funeral director services: $1,500
- casket: $2,300
- embalming: $500
- use of funeral home for funeral service: $500
- gravesite: $1,000+
- digging the grave: $600
- grave liner or outer burial container: $1,000
- headstone: $1,500

This beautiful copper casket is on the higher end of the price range. Some caskets have inner drawers for family to place keepsakes in, such as photos, poems, drawings, small Bibles, etc.

Funeral expenses are either passed down to be paid by family members or are planned for in advance by the individual or family. These expenses are ever-increasing, so locking in the price through some form of preplanning makes economic sense. Being responsible is planning for the inevitable. Various kinds of prearrangement financial options are available, and preplanning has become affordable for many people with prearrangement payment plans, life insurance options, and more. The average funeral expenses are not always all-inclusive. In addition to the burial cost, expect to pay for flowers, honorariums, food, transportation, and more. Many pre-need life insurance companies recommend having at least a $10,000 policy to help cover costs.

Both cheaper and more expensive options are available to consider. Direct cremation eliminates many of the fees, but for many, direct cremation seems impersonal. Most funeral homes now rent caskets to allow people to view a deceased person before cremating the body. These caskets get completely refurbished before renting them again. Others choose direct cremation with an added memorial service with no viewing. There are many options. Preplanning is one of the most loving things anyone could do for their family.

I have thought about these costs a lot of late and have determined in my own heart that they are fair and, in many cases, a bargain for what people receive. My wife and I recently made prearrangements. I discovered that a used automobile could easily cost more than the average prearrangement. Most people do not look at it like that yet when surprised by the death of a loved one, they become unnecessarily stressed due to cost shock.

Caskets are available in many styles and colors. This casket is rented for a viewing prior to a cremation. After the cremation, this casket is completely refurbished to be rented again.

Chapter Four

HOW TO DELIVER A GREAT SERVICE

In this chapter, I've included Celebrations of Life for Charles Lee Potts and Alice Senderpost (pseudonyms). When delivering a celebration of life, the headings provided are not spoken but are noted here as a reference and to help the officiant keep their place. I have included more detail in the book than I usually do. I've added as much as I deemed necessary to give the reader the best picture of a complete service. I've included two songs and the funeral director's announcements in detail. In the comforting words and Gospel reading sections, I added scripture reading by grandchildren. The purpose is to illustrate how I would incorporate others into the service. If family members do not desire to read, I will read these sections myself. Throughout this chapter, I used fictitious names and locations.

I like to type the entire service into Microsoft Publisher because I prefer a booklet format that is 8.5 inches tall by 5.5 inches wide. This works well for making an excellent little pamphlet or booklet to use. Other programs will also work. For example, a Word document that is 11 inches tall by 8.5 inches wide makes a nice booklet or pamphlet as well.

I usually write a different poem for each service, but hundreds of poems already written are available on the internet. Feel free to use, modify, or rewrite any poem or section in this service to fit your unique style and occasion.

A word of caution: Do not assume that you will remember things that you usually would. A few times when I'd assumed that, I was unable to recall what I needed to. I'd written in just the words, "The Lord's Prayer." When I arrived at that spot in the ceremony, I could not remember how the Lord's Prayer began. My mind went blank for a second, which seemed like an eternity at the time. I finally remembered and continued with the service. I made up my mind not to allow that to happen again. I write the whole thing down. The same rule applies with people. Typically, I have no problem remembering the names of people I am around all the time. I don't know whether it was due to nerves or overthinking, but there have been times when I have forgotten names that should have been obvious and fresh in my mind. For that reason, I write them down. As the old saying goes, "Hope for the best, but prepare for the worst."

| Celebration of Life – First Example

I always start with a title page.

In Loving Memory of

Charles Lee Potts
1931 - 2020
Service at Shady Oak Funeral Home
Committal at Shady Oak Cemetery
Officiant Pastor: Dr. William L. Fix
In Memory of a Life Well Lived

<u>Note</u>:

I printed out the entire service for my staff to teach them how to conduct a service like this. I often use real life situations, such as participating in a memorial service, as a way to teach them. All *other* participants receive the cover page and an order of service to alert them when to speak, sing, read, etc. This was the best way to minimize printing costs while still providing my staff with some excellent training.

Order of Service

Prelude music (pre-recorded)
Funeral director announcement – John the Director
Opening song, "Amazing Grace" pre-recorded
Opening comments – Pastor Bill Fix
Comforting words - Parker Potts
Gospel lesson – Betsy Potts
Prayer and reasons for gathering – Pastor Bill Fix
Eulogy – Pastor Bill Fix
Open sharing – people have an opportunity to share a memory
Poem – Pastor Bill Fix
Sermon – Pastor Bill Fix
The Lord's Prayer – Pastor Bill Fix, leading the congregation
Funeral director's announcement – Director John
Song – "In The Garden" (pre-recorded)
Processional to the cemetery
Graveside service – Pastor Bill Fix
Funeral director's final announcement

Following the order of service, I outline details for each event/part of the service.

Funeral Director's Announcement

Ladies and gentlemen, may I have your attention, please. In just a few moments, Pastor Bill Fix will begin our service for Charles Potts. Out of courtesy to the family and so you do not disturb the service, would you do me a favor and turn off or silence any cell phones? May I also remind you that if you are going to join us in the procession to the committal service at Shady Oak Cemetery, when you return to your cars, please turn on your bright lights and while we are traveling, stay a safe but close distance to the vehicle in front of you. We do have the right of way, but gaps in the procession can cause confusion and a possible accident. Pastor Bill Fix will be the officiant for today's services. Before Pastor Fix begins, the family has chosen a musical selection in honor and memory of Charles.

Song: "Amazing Grace"
Opening Comments by Pastor Bill Fix

On behalf of the Pott's family, I want to thank you for being here today. Your encouragement, along with your cards, flowers, prayers, and kind words, has been comforting to the family. My name is Pastor Bill Fix, and we are here to celebrate the life of Charles Lee Potts. Allow God's Word to be an encouragement and comfort to you today as Charles's fourteen-year-old grandson, Parker, shares a few words of support from the Bible. After Parker, his twelve-year-old sister and granddaughter to Charles, Betsy, will read our Gospel reading for today.

Parker Potts - Words Of Comfort

Jesus said, "Blessed are those who mourn, for they will be comforted." Matthew 5:4

He said, "Peace I leave with you; my peace I give you...Do not let your hearts be troubled and do not be afraid." John 14:27

Jesus said, "I am the resurrection and the life. The one who believes in me will live, even though they die; and whoever lives by believing in me will never die." John 11:25, 26

Betsy Potts - Gospel Reading

Let not your heart be troubled: ye believe in God, believe also in me. In my Father's house are many mansions: if it were not so, I would have told you. I go to prepare a place for you. And if I go and prepare a place for you, I will come again, and receive you unto myself; that where I am, there ye may be also. John 14:1-3 [King James Bible]

Pastor Bill Fix - Prayer

Thank you Parker and Betsy, we are all very proud of you. Would everyone bow your heads as I offer this prayer:

Father in Heaven. Creator of the heavens and the earth. Oh God, we are here today grieving the tremendous loss of a much-loved man, Charles Potts, and to give thanks to you for his life among us. We mourn today over how different our lives will be without him and give thanks to you for how full life was when he was with us. As we consider the shortness and uncertainty of life on earth, we also give thanks to you for the gift of eternal life and the gift of family and the gift of friendships. Lord, we ask that you would comfort us this day as we come together to share our love and sweet memories with one another. In Jesus's name, we pray, Amen.

Prayer and Reasons for Gathering – Pastor Bill Fix

There are three good reasons why we have come here today:

- To remember a good life – Charles Potts's Life
- To comfort and encourage one another – Charles's friends, relatives, work associates, neighbors.
- To cling to the promises of God found in His Word

Eulogy

Charles Lee Potts was born January 10, 1931 in Waynesboro, Pennsylvania. He went to his eternal rest March 28, 2020. He was eighty-nine years old or young, whichever way you look at it.

Eighty-nine years may seem like a long time for many of you, but in comparison to all eternity, it is just a short time.

Charles is preceded in death by:

- His parents, Mark and Melissa Potts
- His loving and faithful wife of fifty-two years, Kattie Potts
- His daughter, Kimberly Potts
- And another daughter, Charlene Potts
- His brother, Frank Potts married to Cora, who is with us today

Surviving Charles are two sons and a daughter

- A son, Kenneth and his wife, Beverly Potts
- A son, Heath and his wife, Stephanie Potts
- A daughter, Shannon and her husband, Joe Poncracz (pronounced Poncrass)

Surviving Charles are two beloved brothers and a sister

- A brother, John and his wife, Alva Potts
- A brother, Bill and his wife, Jane Potts
- A sister, Maryann married to the late Edward Filder

Surviving Charles are five beautiful grandchildren

- Darol, Haley, Parker, Katie, and Owen

Surviving Charles are two precious great-grandchildren

- Isabella and Olivia

Surviving Charles are many cousins, nieces, and nephews that have been influenced by his love and life.

What a tremendous legacy Charles leaves in his family. Let's give him a round of applause.

I asked some family members to meet with me and tell me about Charles's life. They gave me one- and two-word phrases that describe Charles. They described him as:

- <u>Kind and loving</u>. When a family member was going through a hard time financially, Charles would buy them a bag of groceries and put an additional one hundred dollar bill in the grocery bag. Kimberly, his daughter, said that he was the most kind and loving dad any person would ever want.

- <u>A very generous person</u>. He didn't have to buy the groceries and give the extra hundred dollars, but he did it anyway. He used to get up at 4 a.m. to pick his brother up at work before his brother was able to buy a car. He was generous to a fault. He would often stop and talk with people holding signs that read "Will work for food." He would often give them money but more often bring them back a meal from Wendy's or McDonald's.

- <u>An organized person</u>. Everything had its place, especially his tools. He knew where every one of his tools belonged. When the boys secretly used his tools, they mysteriously ended up in a different spot, yet he knew they had been using his tools.

- <u>A lot of fun</u>. He liked riding the four-wheeler on the paths up north. He enjoyed the all-night Monopoly games full of wheeling and dealing. He loved to go to the state fairs with his grandchildren.

- <u>Outspoken</u>. If he thought it, he was probably saying it. Charles had your back and stood up for people he loved. You knew you could take any problem to him, and he would be upfront with you, then he would help you fix it if he could. Someone once said something admirable about Charles: "Many people fix the blame, but Charles fixed the problem." He was a problem solver, not just a problem finder.

- Best dad, best grandpa, best uncle, best friend.

- His grandson Parker told me his grandpa was <u>a fighter</u>. He had been on life support but wanted it removed. For nine hours, he fought to live without life support. He fought the battle of his life.

- Shannon's husband Joe told me Charles had <u>the heart of a rhino</u>.

- <u>A peacemaker</u>. Shannon said her dad hated conflict. He always tried to make people feel happy One Sunday, as they were going somewhere, Shannon was upset. Charles wanted to know why and she told him because she was going to miss church. "You will not," he said, then put on a suit and took her to church.

- His sons told me he wanted them to do the right thing, and he would nudge them in the right direction. If they didn't go that way, he pushed them to make the right decision. If they still would not do the right thing, he would push harder, putting the boot to the booty when they needed it.

Education

- Charles was a graduate of Waynesboro High School in Wanesboro, Pennsylvania.
- His education continued in the Army.
- He continued to learn when he got married to Katie.
- He learned a lot working for Ford Motor Company.
- Having kids of his own was a learning experience too.
- Having grandkids, then great grandkids was also a learning experience.
- He was a life-long learner.

Armed services

- Charles was in the Army during the Korean conflict.
- He joked a lot about being in the Army and had many exciting stories.

Employment

- Charles worked at Ford Motor Company until he retired at sixty-seven.
- Cass and Ronald, coworkers with Charles at Ford, said he was a no-nonsense, hard worker; talkative, stubborn and opinionated.

Health issues

- Charles had chronic obstructive pulmonary disease, a ruthless disease.
- He had severe hearing loss and a cochlear implant. The hearing loss was from the sound of guns in the Army.
- He recently expressed that he was ready and desired to go home.

Charles loved many things:

- He loved working with his hands; he did carpentry and was quite a mechanic.
- Charles was not a real sports fan but liked being outdoors.
- He was fantastic with kids and had a calming effect on them.
- He loved his family; precious pictures prove this.
- His wife: Charles and Katie were married in 1968.
- Family reunions and get-togethers.

Pictures displayed around the room. They say a picture is worth a thousand words, and some beautiful pictures are displayed in this room today. Every photo represents a moment in time. Each little snapshot is a memory to grasp.

- A happy time with daughter, Charlene, and her horse
- A real keepsake, a family reunion picture in Pennsylvania
- The family farm with Charles and his brothers, sister, and their dogs
- Charles standing beside his brother Bill
- Katie and Charles's wedding pictures—did they ever look sharp!
- Wedding picture of Katie and their mothers
- Charles with a grandson, holding a couple of fishing poles
- A granddaughter's graduation
- Mother of his great-grandchildren
- Many special moments with grandchildren and great-grandchildren, Isabella and Olivia
- Family celebration with balloons and a picture of a moose behind a large group of people, many smiles

Open Sharing - Poem

As I prepared to speak to you today, I was inspired to write a poem titled "Charles." I hope you like it.

Charles
by Pastor Bill Fix

Charles, you knew how to work real hard
When life would deal a most difficult card
You grew up, and helped work the farm
With its animals and crops and all its charm

Army and Katie and kids and Ford
Life was hard but had a great reward
For the joy, you lived with family and friends
We did not think that someday it would end

Life is full and abundant and fun
Sometimes we walk, more often we run
Worked with your hands; fixed lots of things
Carpenter, mechanic, healer of life's stings

A wonderful man that we will never forget
Although we will miss you, we have not a fret
We know the battle is over, now you are free.
And we are here clinging to every memory.
We love you Charles, Dad, Grandpa, Brother, Neighbor,
    and Friend.

The Sermon — Pastor Bill Fix

God's Word can help us to understand that even in the middle of separation and grief, God has a perfect plan. He loves each of us, even though like sheep we have all gone astray. We mess up.

When we are racing through life and fighting battles, God is with us. I love life, but we undoubtedly experience a lot of pain, sickness, heartache, disappointment, abuse, regret, challenge, hate, and wow! This list is long.

Yet we say life is grand. It is sort of like being invited to eat at the White House to dine with your favorite president. That would be grand. We might put that date on the calendar and circle it because it is important to us. The day finally arrives, and our favorite president sits right next to us. We are famished. We have waited all day for this moment. The Chief of Staff comes in and says to the President, "We have run out of food." It's over. The meal we had planned to eat with the President has suddenly been cut short.

Many times in life, something runs out. Jesus experienced this. He was at a wedding feast with his disciples and his mother. Let me read it to you.

> On the third day, a wedding took place at Cana in Galilee. Jesus' mother was there, and Jesus and his disciples had also been invited to the wedding. When the wine was gone, Jesus' mother said to him, "They have no more wine." "Woman, why do you involve me?" Jesus replied, "My hour has not yet come." His mother said to the servants, "Do whatever he tells you." Nearby stood six stone water jars, the kind used by the Jews for ceremonial washing, each holding from twenty to thirty gallons. Jesus said to the servants, "Fill the jars with water"; so they filled them to the brim. Then he told them, "Now draw some out and take it to the master of the banquet." They did so, and the master of the banquet tasted the water that had been turned into wine. He did not realize where it had come from, though the servants who had drawn the water knew. Then he called the bridegroom aside and said, "Everyone brings out the choice wine first and then the cheaper wine after the guests have had too much to drink; but you have saved the best till now." What Jesus did here in Cana of Galilee was the first of the signs through which he revealed his glory; and his disciples believed in him. John 2:1-11

Points to notice in this passage:

- The wedding feast was in full swing. They were eating and drinking and dancing and having lots of fun. Much of life is like that—fun, full, and fulfilling.

- The wine ran out. Good times seem to run out, like the wine. So does life on earth run its course, and then we breathe our last. No matter how good it may seem, every earthly road ends.

- Jesus put hope back into a hopeless situation Jesus's mother, Mary, knew Jesus could do something. She told the servants to do whatever Jesus said to do. The servants obeyed Jesus. Jesus turned the water into the best wine.

- From his first miracle, Jesus showed us that He saves the best for last.

The same is true in life. When we breathe our last breath here, that's not the end. Our earthly road ends, but the journey continues. Didn't Betsy tell us in her Gospel reading there is a place that Jesus has prepared? Listen to it again.

Let not your heart be troubled: ye believe in God, believe also in me. In my Father's house are many mansions: if it were not so, I would have told you. I go to prepare a place for you. And if I go and prepare a place for you, I will come again, and receive you unto myself; that where I am, there ye may be also. John 14:1-3 [King James Bible]

He has prepared a special place for believers. Jesus saves the best for last. Heaven's description is found and referenced throughout Scripture, but Revelation 21:4 tells us which things will not be there, and I am so glad we have this promise:

"He will wipe every tear from their eyes. There will be no more death or mourning or crying or pain, for the old order of things has passed away." Revelation 21:4

I believe Jesus rescues us from the turmoil of the world. Charles knows all about this place, and it is evident to him today. As we close this portion of our service, will you join me in praying the Lord's Prayer.

The Lord's Prayer

Our Father, which art in heaven, Hallowed be thy name. Thy kingdom come. Thy will be done in earth, as it is in heaven. Give us this day our daily bread. And forgive us our debts, as we forgive our debtors. And lead us not into temptation, but deliver us from evil: For thine is the kingdom, and the power, and the glory, for ever. Amen. Matthew 6:9-13 [King James Bible]

We have concluded services here at the funeral home. John Liken, the funeral director, is now going to provide final instructions.

Funeral Director's Announcement

On behalf of the family, we want to thank you for being here today to remember the life of Charles Lee Potts, and we want to thank Pastor Fix for his warm and kind words. Before we have our final pass-by, if you are going to be driving in the processional to Remembering Gardens Cemetery, we want to remind you to drive with your bright lights on. And do not leave a large gap between you and the car ahead of you as this could cause confusion and may cause an accident. We do have the right away, but we want to caution you to drive safely with your bright lights on and a close, safe distance from the car in front of you. Pallbearers, please remain in the lobby and wait for us there. Before you go to your vehicles, we want to give you one last opportunity to pay your last respects by passing by the casket. My assistants will start dismissing you for the final pass-by beginning in the back of the chapel. Thank you for your kind attention.

Song: "In The Garden"
Processional To The Cemetery

Continuing Service At The Graveside Or Cemetery Chapel

The Lord is my shepherd; I shall not want. He maketh me to lie down in green pastures: he leadeth me beside the still waters. He restoreth my soul: he leadeth me in the paths of righteousness for his name's sake. Yea, though I walk through the valley of the shadow of death, I will fear no evil: for thou art with me; thy rod and thy staff they comfort me. Thou preparest a table before me in the presence of mine enemies: thou anointest my head with oil; my cup runneth over. Surely goodness and mercy shall follow me all the days of my life: and I will dwell in the house of the Lord for ever. Psalms 23:1-6 [King James Bible]

Prayer

Father in Heaven, we have met today to remember the life of Charles Lee Potts. It has felt good to think about the many cherished experiences we've shared with Charles. Thank you, God, for the gift of these memories. Your Word says that you will always be with us, even in the valley of death. Our comfort is in you; our peace is in knowing you are our God; our joy is in knowing that you have conquered the sting of death. Father, your promises that speak to eternal life are many. We cling to these promises today. We proclaim that you are a good and gracious God, and you are with us today. In Jesus's precious name I pray, Amen.

Just for a While
by The People Pastor, Bill Fix

You mourn knowing he has gone from you.
He worked, he played and lived life abundant too.

You imagine him beside you, and you hope that he'll be there.
But when you open your eyes and look around, you see his
empty chair.

Indeed, something is missing, as you look around.
But don't be sad—Charles went home. He's just received
    a crown!

You must go forward, but you know not how.
As you start to function, you will find your smile .

Don't spend your day looking back on the past.
Make many new memories, the kind that will last.

Don't look back and cling only to yesterday.
Be happy for right now and go, live fully!

Cherish the memories you have of his voice .
What you decide to remember will be your choice.

Let his legacy live on, but don't get stuck there.
You need ongoing faith, hope, love and care.

So live in the moment—go ahead and smile .
This separation only lasts for a while.

Closing Prayer

God, as we close this service today, I pray that Charles's family and friends would remember the rich experiences that they have shared. May they talk about Charles often and may they laugh out loud as they remember the good times that they have shared. Comfort them, Father, with a comfort that only you can provide.

For now, to everything that is material: Ashes to ashes, earth to earth and dust to dust, but to the Spirit, we say, now you are free, free of tears, free of pain, free of sickness, free of heartache, free to greet old and new friends and to adventure with them forever. Therefore we say, so long to Charles Potts, until we meet again. In the mighty name of the Father, the Son, and the Holy Spirit. Amen.

Final Announcement - Funeral Director

We have concluded our services for Charles Lee Potts. A luncheon will be held at Baldoso Restaurant immediately following this service. If you need directions to get to the Baldoso, please see one of my associates or myself, and we will be happy to help you. Again, we would like to thank Pastor Fix for his kind words. I want to remind you that this is not goodbye, but so long until we meet again. In just a few moments as you are going back to your car, we will dismiss you from the back to walk by the casket one last time to pay your respects. As you walk by remembering Charles, you can leave your fingerprints behind and take a new memory with you. May God bless each of you as you return to your cars. Be safe as you travel to the luncheon. If there is anything we can do to help you, please see one of us before returning to your vehicle. Thank you!

In older cemeteries, headstones are upright and above ground. Perpetual care is usually included in the purchase of a grave plot. Many cemeteries require that grave markers be flat and lawn-level so riding mowers can be used, facilitating perpetual care.

| Celebration of Life – Second Example

Memorial Service for
Alice Senderpost
1935 – 2020
Officiating Pastor: William L. Fix
Dorigan Funeral Home
Garden of the Angels Cemetery
Services at Taylor Methodist Church

Order of Service

Prelude music before service – Pianist, Linda Hull
"In the Garden" – Terry and Linda Hull
Words of Comfort – Pastor Hankus Powers
Pastoral Prayer – Pastor George Kenderly
Congregational Song – "At the Cross"
Our purpose today – Pastor Bill Fix
Eulogy – Pastor Bill Fix
Congregational Song – "We're Marching to Zion"
Testimony Time – Led by Pastor Matt Sparks
Congregational Song – "Great is Thy Faithfulness"
Message – Pastor Bill Fix
Prayer – Pastor Hubert Rowsling
Graveside Service – Pastor Bill Fix

Prelude Music Before Service – Pianist, Linda Hull
"In The Garden" – Terry and Linda Hull
Words of Comfort – Pastor Hankus Powers

Jesus said, "Let not your heart be troubled: ye believe in God, believe also in me. In my Father's house are many mansions: if it were not so, I would have told you. I go to prepare a place for you. And if I go and prepare a place for you, I will come again, and receive you unto myself; that where I am, there ye may be also." John 14:1-3 [King James Bible]

But I would not have you to be ignorant, brethren, concerning them which are asleep, that ye sorrow not, even as others which have no hope. For if we believe that Jesus died and rose again, even so them also which sleep in Jesus will God bring with him. For this we say unto you by the word of the Lord, that we which are alive [and] remain unto the coming of the Lord shall not prevent them which are asleep. For the Lord himself shall descend from heaven with a shout, with the voice of the archangel, and with the trump of God: and the dead in Christ shall rise first: Then we which are alive [and] remain shall be caught up together with them in the clouds, to meet the Lord in the air: and so shall we ever be with the Lord. Wherefore comfort one another with these words. 1 Thessalonians 4:13-18 [King James Bible]

"Come to me, all you who are weary and burdened, and I will give you rest. Take my yoke upon you and learn from me, for I am gentle and humble in heart, and you will find rest for your souls. For my yoke is easy and my burden is light." Matthew 11:28-30

Pastoral Prayer – Pastor George Kenderly

Lord, we come to celebrate the homegoing of Alice Senderpost. We know You, heavenly Father, as a God of hope, a God of eternity, and a God of all comfort. We come to you today as a people grieving but also thankful. Be near us as we remember Alice and the example she was as a woman with a dynamic faith. Dear Father, help us to have faith as we begin to rejoice that Alice is now with you for all eternity. We are here, Lord, to remember Alice as a caring person, a beloved mother, a precious grandmother, a wonderful great-grandmother, and a much cared about relative and friend. Help us, Father, to remember the good times. May hope well up in us as we reflect on

Alice's eternity. Fill us with your strength and your hope, your joy, your love, and your promise. I pray this in the beautiful name of Jesus. Amen.

Congregational Song – "At The Cross" (Hymn 221)
Our Purpose Today – Pastor Bill Fix

The purpose of our gathering today is not to go through a hollow ceremony. It is not simply to attend another funeral for someone we love. No, we are here for at least three excellent reasons:

- To remember a good lady, a good life, a precious person who will be greatly missed.—Alice. A hard worker, an encourager, a generous person and a sister in the Lord.

- We are here to comfort one another: the friends, relatives, neighbors, and work associates of Alice sense a significant loss with her passing. She was a Christian comrade, Alice Senderpost. I want to encourage you to follow up and talk about Alice to those grieving the most today. Grief isn't over in a day, and this close family's matriarch has graduated to Heaven, and they miss her.

- We are here to cling to the promises of God and to the eternal hope that we have in knowing Jesus as Savior. Alice was a Christ follower; she knew Jesus as her Lord and Savior. She believed He was the only way to Heaven. She knew him as the door or gateway to heaven. She believed Jesus when he said, "I am the door," and Alice knew the Way for she knew that Jesus has said, "I am the way, the truth, and the life, no man comes to the Father except by me."

Eulogy

A celebration in remembrance of Alice E. Senderpost. Her son, Dale said it best: Mom has perfect vision in both eyes. She can now walk without a walker and without assistance. She can run, and jump, and dance. She has great freedom. She has countless friends and relatives with her now. More than she had while she was here with us. She has genuinely entered her promised land. She now has a home in gloryland that outshines the sun. She is with Jesus. Amen!

Alice was born July 4, 1935, in Ontario, Canada.

She went to be with the Lord, on July 12, 2020.

Just a few days ago on July 4, she celebrated her eighty-fifth birthday complete with birthday cake, surrounded by family.

Alice had another birthday—her spiritual birthday—the day she gave her life to Jesus. Alice told me a few nights ago she was saved by Jesus at age five in Sunday School. She made a deeper commitment to the Lord at age twenty-one. Alice has gone home to Heaven.

Alice is preceded in death by:

- her mom and dad, Ralph and Mary Smith
- her sisters Dorothy, Arlene, and Mary.
- her loving husband of almost fifty years, Arlando.

Alice is survived by:

- her son, Dale Senderpost and his wife, Sharon.
- a daughter, Janet Sherief, married to David.
- five grandchildren: Michelle DeFanta, Lisa Senderpost; Dawn Wildman, married to James; Gayle Clobb, married to Darin; and Julie Franklinson, married to Ray.
- ten great-grandchildren: Meagan Joy, Caris Elizabeth, Sophia Grace, Drew Samuel, Zachary Taylor, Bethany Joy, Sean (Shawn), Sidney, Spenser, and Olivia

Alice was always active in the church

- As a Sunday School teacher
- On boards and committees
- Singing in the choir
- Acted as greeter, evangelist, promoter, inviter, and treasurer

Alice always had a sparkle in her eye, almost childlike

- Many adults lose that sparkle. Alice hadn't.
- A pastor said the sparkle in children's eyes was the light of Christ.
- Alice had that twinkle—she had the light of Christ in her eyes.

Her sense of humor was not loud and boisterous, but still present. If you weren't listening, you'd miss it.

As her pastor, I would often kiss her on the forehead as I said goodbye. Then, I would say sorta tongue-in-cheek, "Now, don't tell my wife." Her reply always made me laugh inside. "I'll not say a word." Most of the time, my wife was standing right there, hearing it all.

Jackie Burnette of Lincoln Park credited Alice for inviting to attend church. Jackie would often drop off the kids and go on about her business. Alice caught her one day and said, "Next week, instead of just dropping the kids off, why don't you stay?" And so, Jackie promised her she would, and she did. And she rededicated her life to Christ. Jackie is still involved. She went on to serve on their Board of Directors, as a piano player, and more. Alice was a great promoter of her church.

Dale said he remembered his mom singing the hymn, "Sunlight, sunlight, in my soul today. Sunlight, sunlight, all along the way. Since the Savior found me, took away my sin, I have had the sunlight of His love within." What a great memory. Do you think there is a homecoming reunion in heaven right now? I do.

When I spoke to Alice and shared with her one of my favorite songs, "We're Marching to Zion," she said it was one of her favorites too. I recited a few lines of that song, and then she recited a few lines. In a little while, we are all going to sing, "We're Marching to Zion."

For sixty-nine years, Alice Senderpost was a very hard worker. She graduated from high school in 1947, attended Boston College, worked for a team of three doctors, worked for Dr. Dan Hermir, worked for Dr. W.P. Stark, and worked fourteen years for Stargon Realty.

Alice would walk the seven blocks to work, walk home to prepare lunch for the kids, walk back to work and walk home at night.

When Dale and Janet were teens, Alice would give them chores to do. They were not always in a hurry to complete those chores. Alice would call Arlando and tell him to come home because Dale and Janet were not working very hard on their tasks. Dale would call his dad and tell him to take the long way home—more than seven blocks. That usually gave them enough time to get the chores done.

Dale told me that the night he got married, his mother, Alice, was ironing his shirt and had tears in her eyes. Dale asked, "What's wrong, Mom?" She said, "I just realized I am ironing your shirt for the last time."

Janet told me that her Mom was not only a hard worker, but she was also a good worker and had a great work ethic. She took life seriously.

Alice believed she had received her marching orders. A few months before she went to be with the Lord, she had told me that she'd had a rough night, and she was wondering to herself, *Is this what it is like to die?* I told her the process of dying is often complicated but it did not hurt to die, at least for a Christian. Apostle Paul asked, "Where, O death, is your sting?" (1 Corinthians 15:55). The Bible says that to be absent from the body is to be present with the Lord (2 Corinthians 5:8). Paul had often thought in his latter years that it would be a far better thing to go on and be with the Lord. Likewise, Alice had received her marching orders.

> She was marching to Zion,
> beautiful, beautiful Zion.
> She was marching upward to Zion,
> the beautiful city of God.

"We're Marching to Zion" — Congregational Song

Think about Homecoming. Alice has arrived in Heaven. Can you imagine what she might say?

"Hello Arlando, I have missed you! Oh, Mary, my precious sister, and Herb, it is good to be with you. Mom, Dad, relatives, and friends.

Wait, there's the Lamb of God—Jesus! I...I...I'm going to bow down and worship Him."

What a homecoming! God is so faithful.

"Great Is Thy Faithfulness" — Congregational Song

Alice had walked with Jesus many times. She would always take Him home to her house. The other night as they were walking along life's highway, Jesus took her home to His house, the place He had prepared for her.

Alice loved Scripture. One of her favorite passages was Isaiah 40:28-31.

> *"Do you not know? Have you not heard? The Lord is the everlasting God, the creator of the ends of the Earth. He will not grow tired or weary and his understanding no one can fathom. He gives strength to the weary and increases the power of the weak. Even youths grow tired and weary and young men stumble and fall; but those who hope in the Lord will renew their strength. They will soar on wings like eagles; they will run and not grow weary, they will walk and not be faint." Isaiah 40:28-31*

When I was meditating on the first line of this Scripture, "Do you not know? Have you not heard?" the Lord reminded me of an old song we used to sing that answers these questions.

Everybody Ought to Know

Everybody ought to know, Everybody ought to know,
Everybody ought to know, Everybody ought to know
Who Jesus is.

Everybody ought to know, Everybody ought to know,
Everybody ought to know, Who Jesus is.

He's the Lily of the Valley, He's the Bright and Morning Star;
He's the fairest of ten thousand, Everybody ought to know.

Everybody ought to know, Everybody ought to know,
Everybody ought to know, Who Jesus is.

On the cross He died for sinners, And His blood makes white
as snow;
Loving, living, coming Savior, He's the one you ought to know.

Everybody ought to know, Everybody ought to know,
Everybody ought to know, Who Jesus is.

Everybody ought to know, Everybody ought to know,
Everybody ought to know, Who Jesus is.

Most things created and sought after in life are wood, hay and stubble to be burned up in the end, but the Lord, He is the everlasting God. He is the creator of everything. He does not get tired or weary (as we do). He understands everything. He gives strength to the weary and increases power of the weak.

Those who hope in the Lord will renew their strength. They will soar on wings like eagles. They will run and not grow weary. They will walk and not grow faint.

Yea, though I walk through the valley of the shadow of death, I will fear no evil: for thou art with me. Psalms 23:4 [King James Bible]

Prayer

Father, we have met and remembered the extraordinary life of Alice Senderpost. We have smiled at the stories, and we celebrate her going home to be with you. We do not grieve as those who have no hope. We know that a good woman has gone on and will be missed by many. Comfort this family, Father. Speak to their hearts and remind them that you will never leave them nor forsake them. I pray this in Jesus's name. Amen.

Graveside Service

Jesus said, "Blessed are those who mourn, for they will be comforted." Matthew 5:4

He also said, "Peace I leave with you; my peace I give you...Do not let your hearts be troubled and do not be afraid." John 14:27

God's Word says,

"When you pass through the waters, I will be with you; and when you pass through the rivers, they will not sweep over you. When you walk through the fire, you will not be burned; the flames will not set you ablaze. For I am the Lord your God, the Holy One of Israel, your Savior." Isaiah 43:2-3

Lord's Prayer

Our Father, which art in heaven, Hallowed be thy name. Thy kingdom come. Thy will be done in earth, as it is in heaven. Give us this day our daily bread. And forgive us our debts, as we forgive our debtors. And lead us not into temptation but deliver us from evil: For thine is the kingdom, and the power, and the glory, for ever. Amen. Matthew 6:9-13 [King James Bible]

The Lord is my shepherd; I shall not want. He maketh me to lie down in green pastures: he leadeth me beside the still waters. He restoreth my soul: he leadeth me in the paths of righteousness for his name's sake. Yea, though I walk through the valley of the shadow of death, I will fear no evil: for thou art with me; thy rod and thy staff they comfort me. Thou preparest a table before me in the presence of mine enemies: thou anointest my head with oil; my cup runneth over. Surely goodness and mercy shall follow me all the days of my life: and I will dwell in the house of the Lord for ever. Psalms 23:1-6 [King James Bible]

Afterglow
by Helen Lowrie Marshall

I'd like the memory of me to be a happy one
I'd like to leave an afterglow of smiles when life is done.
I'd like to leave an echo, whispering softly down the ways,
of happy times and bright sun shiny days.
I'd like the tears of those who grieve to dry before the sun
As you remember happy memories, I leave when life is done.

Final Prayer

Lord, I want to thank you for the extraordinary life Alice lived, all 85 years of them. I want to thank you for this family: Dale, Sharon, Janet and Dave, and the grandchildren and great-grandchildren; may they too live long, prosperous lives. May they have good memories when they remember Alice and may they talk about her for the rest of their lives. Give them strength to continue living their life according to your will. Amen.

And now, according to the eternal plan, the body returns to the earth as it was, and the spirit to God who gave it. Of all that is material, we say earth to earth, ashes to ashes, dust to dust, but to the Spirit we say, "Now, thou art free from the pain, grief, sickness, and the sorrow of this life. You are free from physical handicaps, free to greet old and new friends, and to adventure with them forever." Therefore we say goodbye to Alice E. Senderpost. Goodbye until we meet again, In the mighty name of the Father, Son, and Holy Ghost. Amen.

Final Announcement - Funeral Director

Urns are used to house cremains. Cremains are sometimes placed in a mausoleum or columbarium, buried at a cemetery, or stored in a home or church. Cremains may be scattered in accordance with applicable state guidelines.

| The Most Difficult Services

Every life is precious and significant and loved by God. The people who remain grieve at the loss of someone they love. All services are hard to various degrees. Some services are more complicated than others because of the circumstances and the emotional connection that the officiant has with the deceased or the deceased's family. The death of a young parent, an only child, a twin, a younger brother or sister, or the last living relative from any generation is hard. The most difficult memorial service for me is for an infant or young child.

Infant and child services are the toughest for many reasons:

- Parents of a deceased child are devastated by the child's death. They often tell me the same thing: "It seems so wrong to bury a child." They always expect to die before their child. Burying a child is the hardest thing they have ever done.

- A young infant has a minimal past to talk about and a child has developing interests.
- An infant's faith is not much to be spoken of and a young child may or may not have had childlike faith. Something positive to say about the parents' faith may or may not be present.
- Parents often ask, "How can a loving God allow a little defenseless child to die?"
- Many of the songs, scriptures, and promises in adult's and children's services are the same.

Preparing for infant and young child services is difficult but I have done them and offer the following pointers:

- Much can be said about the love and faithfulness of God, and this is a great place to begin.
- Although the infant had more time in the womb than in the world, the infant is now experiencing eternity with God.
- Not much can be noted about anything the infant did. The baby never worked anywhere, never went to school, never danced, played sports, married, had a hobby, or even a pet. Still, there is much to remember. The parents will remember holding their baby.
- Many things unique about this child include the child's little hands, feet, mouth, and ears; the baby's eyes, the baby's cry, and the baby's warmth.
- The baby still had many unique traits. The baby breathed rapidly, a bond developed, love grew, and a name was given.
- Indeed, God was with this child and all the promises of God are true.

"See that you do not despise one of these little ones. For I tell you that their angels in heaven always see the face of my Father in heaven." Matthew 18:10

The baby:

- Had a guardian angel that was always looking at the face of God
- Never understood all of the harmful negative media
- Never felt the pain of rejection
- Never mourned separation
- Was never bullied by a bunch of kids
- Never went out drinking
- Never did drugs and was not lost due to an overdose of heroin
- Was pure and holy

Chapter Five

HOW TO AVOID COMMON MISTAKES

The following common errors should be avoided in order to ensure the service runs smoothly.

Mispronouncing names

I have learned the importance of pronouncing names correctly. People get angry, disappointed, and upset at the mispronunciation of names. Pronouncing someone's name wrong is one of the most common mistakes made. If the officiant mispronounces a name, the family and close friends of the deceased will have trouble hearing anything else. Every name mentioned is significant, especially to the person with that name. Taking the time to get these details correct is an indication that the officiant has taken the time to know the family. When meeting with family members, the officiant discusses the proper pronunciation of all names.

Ignoring a nickname

If a person's name is William but everyone calls them Bill, use Bill. If a person never uses their formal name, the officiant shouldn't use it very often either. Use the name everyone called them, the name most commonly used. My cousin, James, was always called Jimmy. I performed a funeral for a person who had a nickname, but I didn't know it. At the close of the service, someone yelled out, "That was a nice service, but we always called him Jack." I had no clue. No one had said anything about this nickname when I met with his family, and it was not on any of the funeral home documents. How would I know? Since this experience, I always ask the question, "Did they have any nicknames?"

Assuming gender

Names like Terry and Jamie can be either female or male. The officiant who believes Terry and Jamie are boys may be incorrect. A gender mistake can easily be prevented by meeting with and getting to know the family before the service.

Being too generic

Speaking in generalities about the deceased instead of being specific and personal is a colossal error. One of the three reasons for having a service is to remember the life of the person. Individualization or personalization requires knowing the specifics about the person instead of generalities. The best way to learn about a person you have never met is through those who loved them the most. Meeting with the family and asking questions about the deceased is the best way to gather personal information. Information collected in the family meeting along with experiences with the person provided by friends and relatives offers a plethora of eulogy information. Another way to learn about the person is to examine the pictures the family chose to display at the funeral home. Photos show events, gatherings, graduations, marriages, sports activities, interests, and other details about the person's life.

Not using humor

The best services are those that present life in the full realm of emotions and responses. We experience joy, laughter, love, peace, excitement, hope, faith, and other positive feelings throughout life. If life includes these emotions, then it is plausible that the eulogy should also include these things. Some officiants make the mistake of omitting the humor and positive feelings in life. Most families would rather hear about the excellent experiences of the deceased then about the last six months of cancer with unbearable pain and suffering. The pain and suffering have their place in the service, but to dwell there would serve an injustice to the family.

Tommy, my nephew, came to me as a teen and said, "Uncle Billy, when I die, I want you to read my eulogy. You will like it. It's hilarious. People will crack up." Tommy had muscular dystrophy and knew his time was short. When he died, his desire had been for people to remember the smiles he'd given and received in life and not the constant battle he fought with muscular dystrophy.

Allowing the service to go too long

The proper length of a memorial service is dependent upon the elements included in it. A one-hour service is acceptable but lengthy. Memorial services with multiple songs, open microphones, a military tribute, etc, can go too long. Determining exactly how long each of these elements will take is impossible. Without these variables, a service will generally be twenty to thirty minutes in length. Everything added increase this time. Going too long is a common mistake. People are more apt to listen and absorb a shorter service than a longer one. I recommend not exceeding an hour.

Preaching a person into or out of Heaven

Communicate the truth of the Gospel the best you can under the circumstances you have. It is not necessary to determine the spiritual condition of the individual. Someone once told me there would be three surprises in heaven: some people you thought would be there are *not*; some people you thought would not be there *are*; and *you* are there. Preach the hope we have in the Lord. The day I realized the service was not for the deceased but for family and friends of the deceased was an eye-opening day. Preach the Word and share the promises of God with the survivors. To the best of your ability with the parameters set by the family, try to proclaim the extent of God's love. To miss this opportunity is a colossal mistake. God's Word will not return void.

Preaching a person into or out of heaven is a mistake officiants often make. We can and should hear and give testimony to the fruit of one's labor, their profession of faith, and the gentleness of their character. When we do, it is easy for us to picture them in Heaven with the Savior. When the family is non-religious or even hostile to the Bible,

I have quoted the words of one of the greatest kings of Israel, who said in Psalms 23, "The Lord is my Shepherd, I shall not want." I am known to quote Solomon, the wisest man who ever lived, who said, "There is a time for everything, and a season for every activity under the heavens: a time to be born and a time to die." I often share about one of the greatest self-sacrificing leader of all time, Jesus, who said, "Greater love hath no man than this, that a man lay down his life for his friends." In a believer's service, I can openly speak of Jesus, who came to abolish death and give us eternal life, but in a nonbeliever's service, I share truth differently.

Failing to be flexible

Despite the many unusual requests, in all instances, try to be Christlike. A song selection may not seem appropriate but may have a special meaning to the surviving family. These selections seem unusual but I usually allow it. The family may desire military services be held before the officiant speaks. A different order of service may seem more appropriate but in reality, it does not matter. If the family wants something different or unusual, I usually go along with it, if I can.

Reinventing the wheel

Using a message previously shared at another service in your sermon is perfectly acceptable. I often preach Psalms 23—like any good story, it gets better with the telling. Added touches, such as memorizing the scripture, use of alliteration, etc., make the message better. When called upon to remember a life, I feel comfortable enough to preach about a dozen or so passages. I spend time comforting the family, learning about the deceased's life, and often allow the family to choose the Scriptures they would like me to use in the message. A favorite scripture like Matthew 5 or Philippians 4:13 is easily adapted into a message. What changes the most from funeral to funeral is the eulogy. The Scripture may be chosen based on each situation. To craft an entirely new service using different comforting words, poems, scriptures, and sermon for a different graveside is a lot of unnecessary work. Even the eulogy has common elements: birthdate and place, date of death, surviving relatives, relatives preceding in death, hobbies, education, work history, favorite things, things remembered for, faith statement, etc. Reinventing the wheel is not necessary when crafting the service. Proven methods have been proven to work. Become familiar with the most frequently used scriptures. My list begins with Psalms 1 and 23; John 2, 14:1-6, and 11:25-26; and Matthew 5.

Failing to open strong

Begin with a powerful and profound statement like, "We are here today to remember the good life of John William Smith (formal name of the deceased)." Share a strong promise of scripture, such as, "I am the resurrection, and the life: he that believeth in me, though he were dead, yet shall he live: And whosoever liveth and believeth in me shall never die" (John 11:25-26, King James Bible). A strong beginning sets up the service as no-nonsense, powerful, and filled with hope. To do otherwise would be a grave mistake.

Failing to pray with focus

Prayer can become mechanical words, meaningless and almost unheard. Or they can be powerful, meaningful, and deep-rooted in scripture. All of the prayers used in a service should be scripted, or thought through in advance. Giving thought to each prayer allows the clergy or officiant time to craft words of deep personal meaning and to recognize a loving and caring God with gratitude, need and thanksgiving. Prayers should give thanks for life, God's presence, and eternal hope. To pray otherwise opens the door for the prayer to be irrelevant or irreverent. When we pray corporately, we need to remember we are speaking more than mere words but from our heart to an all-powerful, all-knowing, ever-present, omniscient God.

Failing to recognize caregivers

Failure to mention the compassion and care the deceased received from others would be negligent. The family may want to thank the doctors and nurses, a particular family member, a caregiver, a church, hospice staff, or some other person or group for being there for the deceased in a difficult time. When meeting with the family, you can ask the question, "Are you especially grateful for any person or group of people, who cared for your loved one during their fiercest battles?" Include the people they mention in the eulogy.

Inappropriate receipt of an honorarium (voluntary payment)

Receive all honorariums with grace. Joking about a remuneration publicly or privately is a mistake. Indicate thankfulness. If the family gives you a card or an envelope, this is an excellent time to extend an invitation for them to call you anytime if they need to talk or could use your services. I often tell the family that if anyone has a difficult time that I am available for counseling or to chat over a cup of coffee. Rarely do family members need additional advice but genuinely making the offer is appropriate. Giving an honorarium can be handled inappropriately as well. Once, I was embarrassed by a funeral home employee who handed me an envelope containing a check and said, "You have been waiting for this—don't spend it in one place." Funeral directors are much more discrete and hand me the envelope privately, thanking me for my services. When I receive an extra amount of money beyond what was expected from a family member because they loved the service and the extraordinary care I provided, I always remind them that I had already received an honorarium. When they tell me they want to give me more, I graciously accept.

Joking with funeral home staff before the service

I know many of the staff at the funeral homes in and around my community. I am always cordial but careful not to stand around and joke with them before the service. A cordial handshake or hug is fine but the family may consider laughing and joking with the staff as irreverent or inappropriate.

Allowing an open microphone when not approved

The decision to open up the microphone for people attending the funeral to say a few words about the deceased or to comfort the family is a decision I always leave up to the family. Time constraints may restrict this option. If people are waiting at the burial site for military honors or if the burial site staff leave at a set time, then the family needs to be aware of those restrictions before opening up the mic. The possibility of inappropriateness at an open microphone always exists. At one service, a son who was angry with his deceased dad vented his anger toward his dad instead of saying positive things. At another, a motorcycle gang talked about their open alcohol and drug use. People have at times used all kinds of vulgarity. Family members have attempted to preach a sermon, often including lengthy, inaccurate use of scripture, sometimes in a cruel manner. The possibility that bad things may be said always exists. The family needs to give me a sign to stop it or stand up and stop it themselves. Open microphone time is usually a very positive thing but the family needs to consider what might go wrong and what others might say. Often the family will select which individuals they'd like to share during this time.

Not knowing the family

Trying to get to know the family just before the funeral is the *last* alternative. Organizing a time to see and talk with the family prior to the service for thirty to sixty minutes is best. Get to know them and allow them time to share information about their loved one. Use these conversations to gather ideas for the service.

Hurried start

Rushing to begin the service before all the family has arrived or people get settled is a mistake and can be disruptive to the service. Allow time for people to be seated and calm before beginning. A funeral director, clergy or celebrant may be the person to indicate when the service is to begin but only after checking with the family.

Arriving late

Arrive before the service to welcome family members and shake hands with those in attendance. Be sure to greet family members by shaking hands and offering encouraging words. Be available to the family in the future by providing them your business card.

Fumbled or forgotten announcements

Forgetting to invite attendees to the reception luncheon or post-service events is a huge mistake. Always confirm the details about where the family would like the congregation to go after the service and remember to warmly invite attendees to the post-service event close to the end of the service. Be sure to confirm whether it is a private gathering for family, invited friends only, or open to everyone.

Appearing irritated

Becoming unsettled when something unexpected pops up is a huge mistake. Something almost always pops up. Funerals are filled with emotions and unexpected requests and experiences can often be brought up. Conflicts may occur, guests may faint, someone may shout, and common courtesy is often forgotten. An excellent exercise is to think through some potential problems and determine how you would respond. This mental preparation can help you to think clearly and act wisely when the unexpected pops up.

Not accepting your limitations

Expecting to have all the answers is too high of an expectation. Having the answer to every question asked is impossible. If you do not know how to answer someone, say so. If you aren't a trained grief counselor, don't attempt to be one! You have the extraordinary task of supporting and guiding a family through a service that helps them to process grief. However, trying to take on grief support after the funeral can put too much on your plate. If you can, be prepared ahead of time with materials, resources, books and support information or be ready to point them in the right direction.

Relying on find-and-replace options in word-processing programs

Automatically replacing the name of the previous person you conducted a funeral for with the name of another person you are doing a service for may be tempting. I was about to do a service for a woman named Beatrice. I decided to use the same format for Beatrice that I'd previously used for Mary, so I directed the program to find all instances of the word "Mary" and replace them with

"Beatrice." I am glad I always read through the service before performing it. Can you imagine me saying, "Beatrice, the Mother of Jesus"? Or what if I'd replaced Al with Fred? Every word that included "al" would be changed to have the word "Fred" in it. The word "although" would become "Fredthough." Not funny at all! Had I not been diligent enough to read through the entire service before presenting it, this could have been very embarrassing. Be careful when using this option. Replace one word at a time instead of replacing them all at once.

Arrogance

Many people do not realize how arrogant they are. We have all seen it and know what it looks like on others. It can be described as an "I am better than you," know-it-all attitude. The pretense of arrogance implies and demands, "I know best, so we will do things my way." A friend of mine sometimes tries to take over the funeral home and tell the funeral director and staff how things are going to be. He is not a good listener and rarely hears the hurt, pain, desires, and regrets of people feeling the grief of loss. He insists on his choice for the scripture, the order of service, and songs. He no longer handles funerals because of his rudeness. Being flexible is of paramount importance. The officiant that quickly gets upset over change will cause an already stressful occasion to become more stressful. Last-minute changes are frequent in this setting. Military service members or veterans who are set to participate in the service may be running late. A family member may be late, and the family will want to wait until they arrive. The music may not play on cue or the microphone may not work. An arrogant officiant cannot handle these inconveniences without expressing anger.

CLOSING REMARKS

I hope this book helps you as you are called upon to conduct a funeral. I am still learning and do not claim to have all the answers. Some denominations would perhaps find this method unorthodox. It has worked well for me and I always do my best. This method for performing memorial services is the method I would like for my Celebration of Life someday.

May God bless you richly and may you serve Him throughout your life. If I can help you or you have a question about the method that I use to conduct funeral services, please email me at fmcbillfix@aol.com. I am known as the People Pastor on Facebook. You can also write to me at:

The People Pastor, Bill Fix
25770 Melody Street
Taylor, Michigan 48180

My first book, *The Dead-End Road Devotional,* is available on Amazon.

Made in the USA
Monee, IL
18 December 2022

22391181R00052